To: ....

From: ....

Find Joy
JOURNAL

SHAUNTI FELDHAHN

iDisciple®

FIND JOY JOURNAL

Find Joy © 2020 by iDisciple LLC.

Scripture quotations, unless otherwise indicated, are taken from the New American Standard Bible®, Copyright © 1960, 1962, 1963, 1968, 1971, 1972, 1973, 1975, 1977, 1995 by the Lockman Foundation. Used by permission. (www.Lockman.org)

Scripture quotations marked ESV are taken from the Holy Bible, English Standard Version®, (ESV®). Copyright © 2001 by Crossway, a publishing ministry of Good News Publishers. Used by permission. All rights reserved.

Scripture quotations marked MSG are taken from The Message. Copyright © 1993, 1994, 1995, 1996, 2000, 2001, 2002. Used by permission of NavPress Publishing Group.

Scripture quotations marked NIV are taken from the Holy Bible, New International Version®. NIV®. Copyright © 1973, 1978, 1984 by Biblica, Inc. All rights reserved worldwide. Used by permission.

Scripture quotations marked NLT are taken from the Holy Bible, New Living Translation, Copyright © 1996. Used by permission of Tyndale House Publishers, Inc., Wheaton, IL 60189 USA. All rights reserved.

Scripture quotations marked RSV are taken from the Revised Standard Version of the Bible, copyright 1952 [2nd edition, 1971] by the Division of Christian Education of the National Council of the Churches of Christ in the United States of America. Used by permission. All rights reserved.

Scripture quotations marked TNIV are taken from the Holy Bible, Today's New International Version®. TNIV®. Copyright © 2001, 2005 by Biblica, Inc. All rights reserved worldwide. Used by permission.

ISBN 978-1-734-95226-1

All quotes taken from Find Joy©

ALL RIGHTS RESERVED

No part of this publication may be reproduced, stored in a retrieval system, or transmitted in any form or by any means – electronic, mechanical, photocopying, recording or otherwise – without the prior written permission.

Requests for information should be addressed to:
iDisciple, 2555 Northwinds Parkway, Alpharetta, Georgia 30009.

Printed in China.

Sisters,

When Jesus was born into our messy, broken world, His arrival was announced by angels who cried, "Fear not, for, behold, I bring you good news of great joy" (Luke 2:10 ESV). Jesus's arrival changed everything. And just as His love for us is not shared only at Christmas, neither is His joy. It is meant to be experienced all year round!

Our world today can seem so uncertain. When everything changes around us, when trials, illnesses, financial challenges, and relationship problems come, we can easily feel the weight of discontent and worry. Yet our God is faithful. He said that He came that we might find joy and life abundant—even in difficulties. It is time to learn how!

We must shift our focus from ourselves and our earthly challenges and instead focus on hearing, seeing, knowing, and trusting our heavenly Father. Change is not always easy. But it is oh so rewarding.

This journal is designed to be a companion to your quiet time, filled with scripture and quotes from the devotional book, *Find Joy: A Devotional Journey to Unshakable Wonder in an Uncertain World*. And as you embark on this journey, I encourage you to take notes, journal your thoughts, write down your memories of God's faithfulness and His presence in your life. Allow Him to guide you on your path to find the good news and great joy that only Christ can give.

Let us receive His joy and pass it on to others.

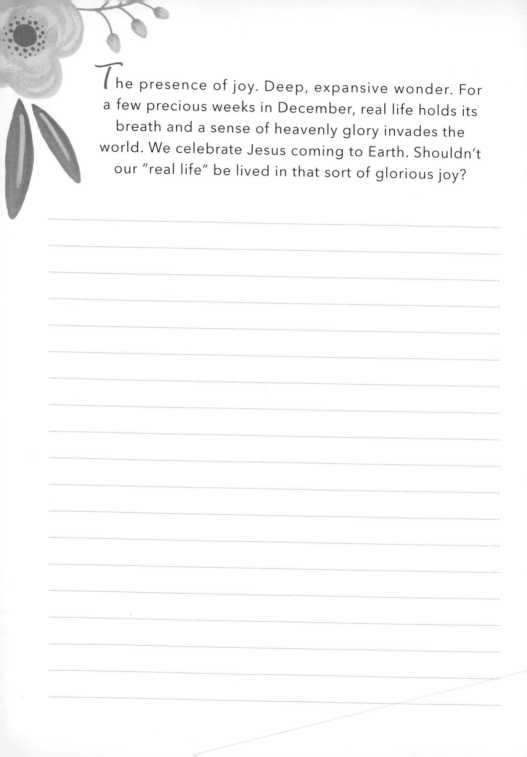

The presence of joy. Deep, expansive wonder. For a few precious weeks in December, real life holds its breath and a sense of heavenly glory invades the world. We celebrate Jesus coming to Earth. Shouldn't our "real life" be lived in that sort of glorious joy?

Without question, this is the great mystery of our faith: Christ
was revealed in a human body and vindicated by the Spirit.
He was seen by angels and announced to the nations. He was
believed in throughout the world and taken to heaven in glory.

1 TIMOTHY 3:16 NLT

*L*ife can be very "real" at times. But so is the
God who has invaded our world! In Him, we
no longer have to struggle under the weight of
condemnation. We can know that at the moment
we step out of this world, we will be running into
the loving arms of the One who created us.

But while he was still a long way off, his father saw him and was filled with compassion for him; he ran to his son, threw his arms around him and kissed him.

LUKE 15:20 NIV

The angels shouted and sang—the news of Jesus's birth was joyous, and He was born with the purpose of bringing us joy.

And the angel said to them, "Fear not, for behold I bring you good news of great joy that will be for all the people. For unto you is born this day in the city of David a Savior, who is Christ the Lord."

LUKE 2:10-11 ESV

*L*et's ask Him to permanently invade our hearts with wonder all year long—and declare that we want to be both recipients and givers of His great joy.

_____

_____

_____

_____

_____

_____

_____

_____

_____

_____

_____

_____

_____

_____

_____

_____

_____

Rejoice always.

1 THESSALONIANS 5:16 ESV

The same God who spoke creation's majesty into being, loves us intimately. He has us and all our problems in His hands.

Therefore let us be grateful for receiving a kingdom that cannot be shaken, and thus let us offer to God acceptable worship, with reverence and awe.

HEBREWS 12:28 ESV

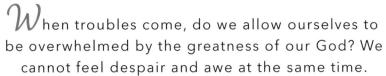

*W*hen troubles come, do we allow ourselves to be overwhelmed by the greatness of our God? We cannot feel despair and awe at the same time.

There is no fear in love, but perfect love casts out fear. For fear has to do with punishment, and whoever fears has not been perfected in love.

1 JOHN 4:18 ESV

*W*hen we truly recognize the awesomeness
of our God, we receive joy in return.

You have turned my mourning into joyful dancing. You have taken away my clothes of mourning and clothed me with joy, that I might sing praises to you and not be silent. O Lᴏʀᴅ my God, I will give you thanks forever!

PSALM 30:11-12 NLT

*W*hat brings success—in activities and in life—is working on and practicing the right things over and over and over. We want to feel joy, peace, and delight, but we aren't always "practicing" the daily habits that lead to that. And one of the crucial elements is gratitude.

Count it all joy, my brothers, when you meet trials of various kinds, for you know that the testing of your faith produces steadfastness. And let steadfastness have its full effect, that you may be perfect and complete, lacking in nothing.

JAMES 1:2-4 ESV

*L*et's practice deep thankfulness that we are intimately loved and cared for by the Creator of the universe.

Come, let us sing for joy to the Lord; let us shout aloud to the Rock of our salvation. Let us come before him with thanksgiving and extol him with music and song. For the Lord is the great God, the great King above all gods.

PSALM 95:1-3 NIV

When we purposely replace negative reactions with a legitimate prayer of gratitude, we live in true joy.

*Do everything without complaining and arguing, so that
no one can criticize you. Live clean, innocent lives as
children of God, shining like bright lights in a world full
of crooked and perverse people.*

PHILIPPIANS 2:14-15 NLT

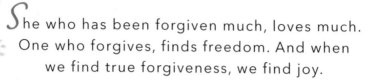

She who has been forgiven much, loves much.
One who forgives, finds freedom. And when
we find true forgiveness, we find joy.

....

....

....

....

....

....

....

....

....

....

....

....

....

....

....

....

....

Put on then, as God's chosen ones, holy and beloved, compassionate hearts, kindness, humility, meekness, and patience, bearing with one another and, if one has a complaint against another, forgiving each other; as the Lord has forgiven you, so you also must forgive.

COLOSSIANS 3:12-13 ESV

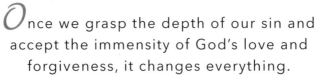

*O*nce we grasp the depth of our sin and
accept the immensity of God's love and
forgiveness, it changes everything.

But he was pierced for our transgressions; he was crushed for our iniquities; upon him was the chastisement that brought us peace, and with his wounds we are healed.

ISAIAH 53:5 ESV

Then God told them what to do once they crossed the Jordan: take stones from the center of the river and pile them where everyone could see. Every time they looked at that cairn, they would remember this astounding thing God did. This was essential because crossing into the Promised Land wasn't the end of the story—it was the beginning.

When your children ask in time to come, "What do those stones mean to you?" then you shall tell them that the waters of the Jordan were cut off before the ark of the covenant of the LORD. When it passed over the Jordan, the waters of the Jordan were cut off. So these stones shall be to the people of Israel a memorial forever.

JOSHUA 4:6-7 ESV

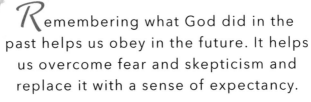

*R*emembering what God did in the past helps us obey in the future. It helps us overcome fear and skepticism and replace it with a sense of expectancy.

Lord, you are my God; I will exalt you and praise your name, for in perfect faithfulness you have done wonderful things, things planned long ago.

ISAIAH 25:1 NIV

$\mathcal{W}$e may have no idea how God will accomplish something He's leading us to do. All we know is that He has something great on the other side. We need to believe God and not our fear, step into the water, and then watch what He does!

....

....

....

....

....

....

....

....

....

....

....

....

....

....

....

But Jesus spoke to them at once. "Don't be afraid," he said. "Take courage. I am here!"

MATTHEW 14:27 NLT

*L*et's watch for each next step.
Then, let us remember. We need to
memorialize His faithfulness!

When you have eaten and are satisfied, praise the LORD your God for the good land he has given you. Be careful that you do not forget the LORD your God, failing to observe his commands, his laws and his decrees that I am giving you this day.

DEUTERONOMY 8:10-11 NIV

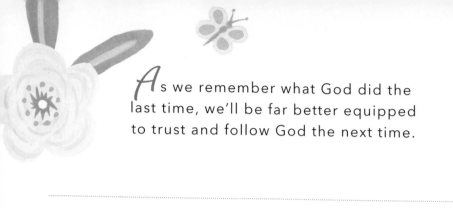

*A*s we remember what God did the last time, we'll be far better equipped to trust and follow God the next time.

I will remember the deeds of the LORD; yes, I will remember your wonders of old. I will ponder all your work, and meditate on your mighty deeds.

PSALM 77:11-12 ESV

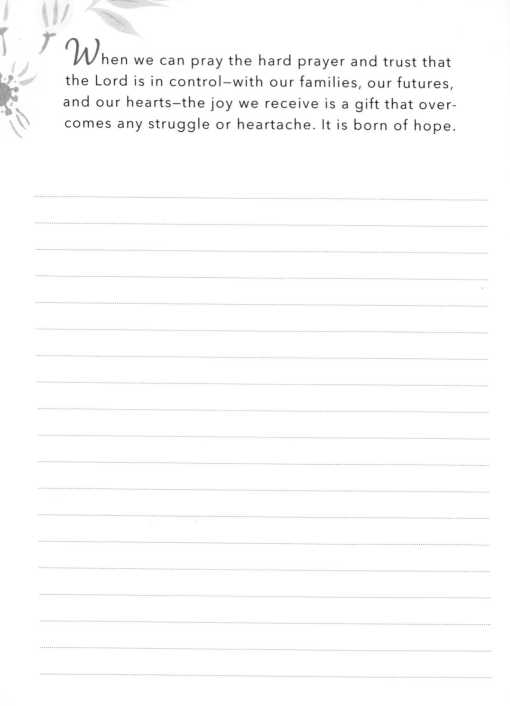

When we can pray the hard prayer and trust that the Lord is in control—with our families, our futures, and our hearts—the joy we receive is a gift that overcomes any struggle or heartache. It is born of hope.

"Blessed is the [woman] who trusts in the LORD, whose trust is the LORD. [She] is like a tree planted by water, that sends out its roots by the stream, and does not fear when heat comes, for its leaves remain green, and is not anxious in the year of drought, for it does not cease to bear fruit."

JEREMIAH 17:7-8 ESV

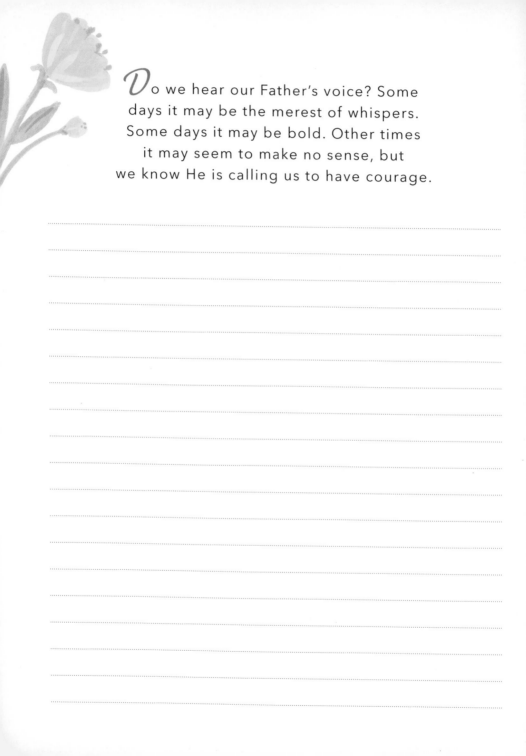

Do we hear our Father's voice? Some days it may be the merest of whispers. Some days it may be bold. Other times it may seem to make no sense, but we know He is calling us to have courage.

But the Helper, the Holy Spirit, whom the Father will send in my name, he will teach you all things and bring to your remembrance all that I have said to you.

JOHN 14:26 ESV

*L*earning the voice of God is a journey, not an event. And we will never hear Him perfectly. But we can listen. We can learn. Then we can leap.

*So faith comes from hearing, that is,
hearing the Good News about Christ.*

ROMANS 10:17 NLT

*J*esus says there is a way to continue to live in that deep feeling of joy: Keep His commandments. He says that as we do so, we will abide in His love and our joy will be full.

*Great peace have those who love your
law; nothing can make them stumble.*

PSALM 119:165 ESV

We are called to keep and guard God's ways out of love, in a world that cries out to us to compromise. We are called to know and hold fast to what He asks of us when our sinful, imperfect hearts are tempted to go our own way.

*The instructions of the L*ORD *are perfect, reviving the soul. The decrees of the L*ORD *are trustworthy, making wise the simple. The commandments of the L*ORD *are right, bringing joy to the heart. The commands of the L*ORD *are clear, giving insight for living.*

PSALM 19:7-8 NLT

$\mathcal{I}$t is usually pretty easy to love ourselves. To keep our own commands and our own counsel. Yet that way won't lead to joy. Jesus tells us what will: loving one another well in His name. Serving those we care about. Treasuring every opportunity to counter our natural tendencies toward stress, irritation, and impatience and instead live out peace, patience, and kindness in front of a watching world.

So if there is any encouragement in Christ, any comfort from love, any participation in the Spirit, any affection and sympathy, complete my joy by being of the same mind, having the same love, being in full accord and of one mind. Do nothing from selfish ambition or conceit, but in humility count others more significant than yourselves. Let each of you look not only to [her] own interests, but also to the interests of others.

PHILIPPIANS 2:1-4 ESV

We can stare at our looming mountain for so long that we take our eyes off of everything else. We lose the big picture. But serving someone else gets us out of ourselves. We are suddenly able to remember that we are the hands and feet of Jesus, serving at His pleasure and willing to be redirected to whichever mountain He chooses that day.

Give, and it will be given to you. Good measure, pressed down, shaken together, running over, will be put into your lap. For with the measure you use it will be measured back to you.

LUKE 6:38 ESV

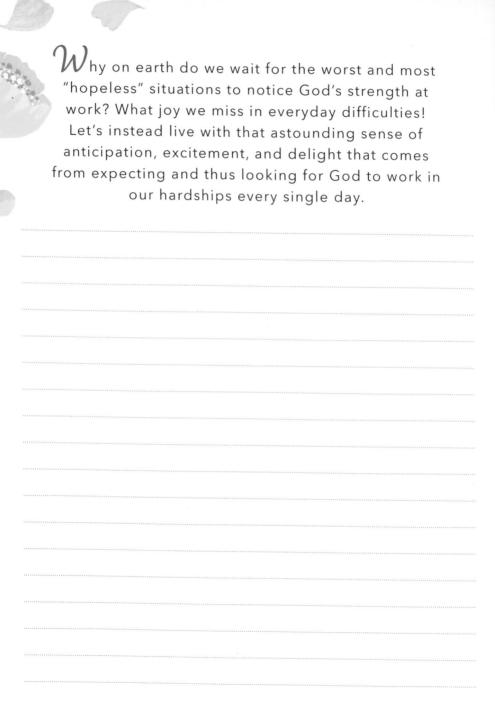

$\mathcal{W}$hy on earth do we wait for the worst and most "hopeless" situations to notice God's strength at work? What joy we miss in everyday difficulties! Let's instead live with that astounding sense of anticipation, excitement, and delight that comes from expecting and thus looking for God to work in our hardships every single day.

Some trust in chariots and some in horses, but we trust in the name of the LORD our God.

PSALM 20:7 ESV

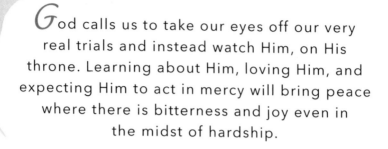

God calls us to take our eyes off our very real trials and instead watch Him, on His throne. Learning about Him, loving Him, and expecting Him to act in mercy will bring peace where there is bitterness and joy even in the midst of hardship.

_____

_____

_____

_____

_____

_____

_____

_____

_____

_____

_____

_____

_____

_____

_____

_____

_____

O LORD of hosts, blessed is the one who trusts in you!

PSALM 84:12 ESV

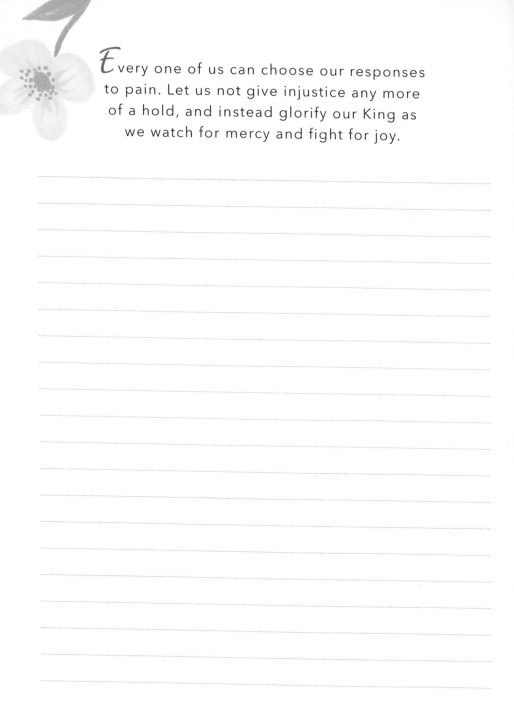

*E*very one of us can choose our responses to pain. Let us not give injustice any more of a hold, and instead glorify our King as we watch for mercy and fight for joy.

[S]he who loves purity of heart, and whose speech is gracious, will have the king as her friend.

PROVERBS 22:11 ESV

[S]he who loves purity of heart, and whose speech
is gracious, will have the king as [her] friend.

PROVERBS 22:11 ESV

As the Father has loved me, so have I loved you. Now remain in my love. If you keep my commands, you will remain in my love, just as I have kept my Father's commands and remain in his love. I have told you this so that my joy may be in you and that your joy may be complete.

JOHN 15:9-11 NIV

$\mathcal{W}$e long for what we see as the promise of Psalm 23, with the shepherd leading the sheep to an immense, soft green lawn. We picture ourselves lying down at our leisure, with everything we need for the foreseeable future. Overabundance. By contrast, we see our own life of faith looking nothing like that.

Trust in the LORD and do good;
dwell in the land and enjoy safe pasture.

PSALM 37:3 NIV

$\mathcal{W}$e become dissatisfied. Or anguished. Because we don't see obvious green fields of provision all around us. But the rocky, dusty, seemingly barren hillside in Israel is what the ancient Israelites called "green pastures"—even though there's no green in sight. Instead, there are tiny tufts of plant life around the base of thousands of rocks, where small amounts of moisture condense. A good shepherd will spot these "green pastures."

And my God will supply every need of yours according to his riches in glory in Christ Jesus.

PHILIPPIANS 4:19 ESV

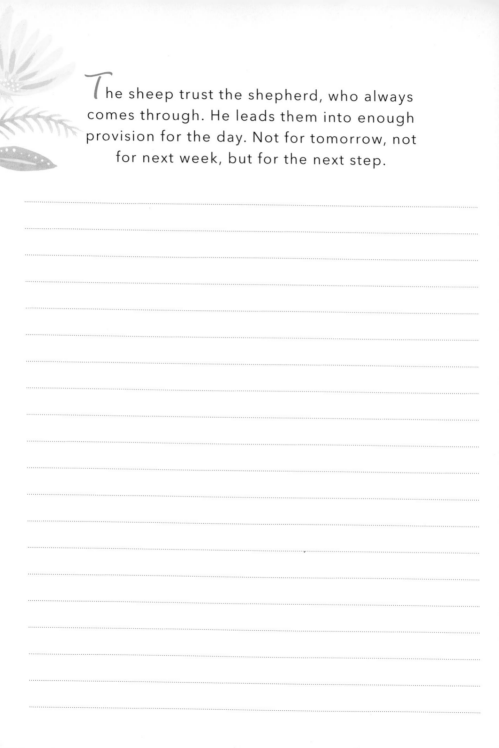

The sheep trust the shepherd, who always comes through. He leads them into enough provision for the day. Not for tomorrow, not for next week, but for the next step.

He tends his flock like a shepherd: He gathers the lambs in his arms and carries them close to his heart; he gently leads those that have young.

ISAIAH 40:11 NIV

Our "will we have enough?" questions can become an adventure; an opportunity to watch God come through. Our good shepherd doesn't mind bringing us to the edge of our fears because He is trying to teach us not to worry about tomorrow. He doesn't seem to stress about delivering in the eleventh hour because He wants, above all, for us to trust Him. To believe that He has the joy of green pastures and still waters for us if we will only see them.

....

....

....

....

....

....

....

....

....

....

....

....

....

....

....

Therefore I tell you, do not worry about your life, what you will eat or drink; or about your body, what you will wear. Is not life more than food, and the body more than clothes? Look at the birds of the air; they do not sow or reap or store away in barns, and yet your heavenly Father feeds them. Are you not much more valuable than they?

MATTHEW 6:25-26 NIV

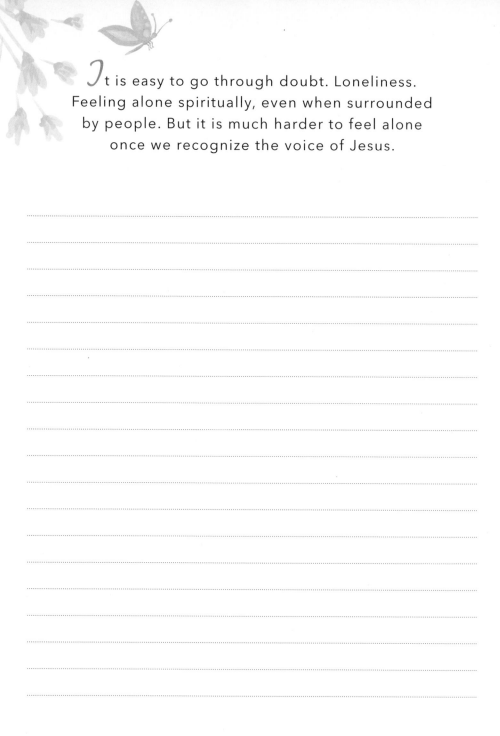

*I*t is easy to go through doubt. Loneliness.
Feeling alone spiritually, even when surrounded
by people. But it is much harder to feel alone
once we recognize the voice of Jesus.

And though the Lord give you the bread of adversity and the water of affliction, yet your Teacher will not hide himself anymore, but your eyes shall see your Teacher. And your ears shall hear a word behind you, saying, "This is the way, walk in it," when you turn to the right or when you turn to the left.

ISAIAH 30:20-21 ESV

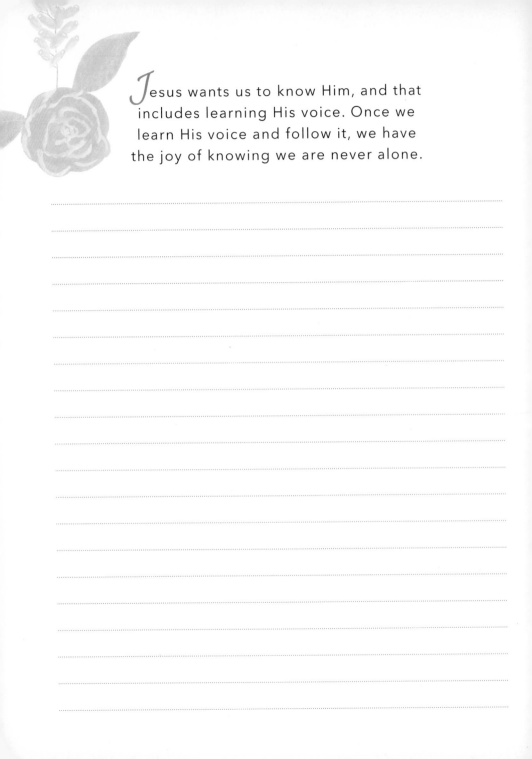

*J*esus wants us to know Him, and that includes learning His voice. Once we learn His voice and follow it, we have the joy of knowing we are never alone.

*Be content with what you have, for he has said,
"I will never leave you nor forsake you." So we
can confidently say, "The Lord is my helper; I will
not fear; what can man do to me?"*

HEBREWS 13:5-6 ESV

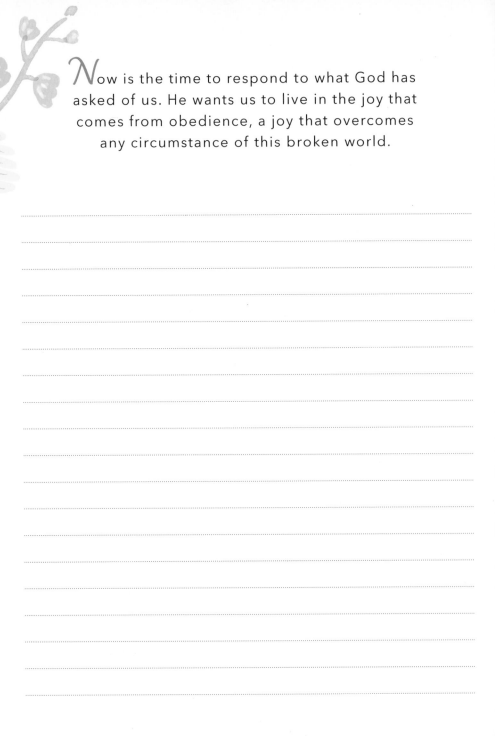

*N*ow is the time to respond to what God has asked of us. He wants us to live in the joy that comes from obedience, a joy that overcomes any circumstance of this broken world.

Therefore, since we are surrounded by so great a cloud of witnesses, let us also lay aside every weight, and sin which clings so closely, and let us run with endurance the race that is set before us, looking to Jesus, the founder and perfecter of our faith, who for the joy that was set before him endured the cross, despising the shame, and is seated at the right hand of the throne of God.

HEBREWS 12:1-2 ESV

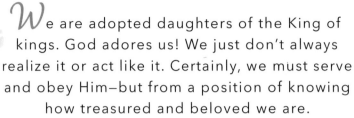

We are adopted daughters of the King of kings. God adores us! We just don't always realize it or act like it. Certainly, we must serve and obey Him—but from a position of knowing how treasured and beloved we are.

Now you are no longer a slave but God's own child.
And since you are his child, God has made you his heir.

GALATIANS 4:7 NLT

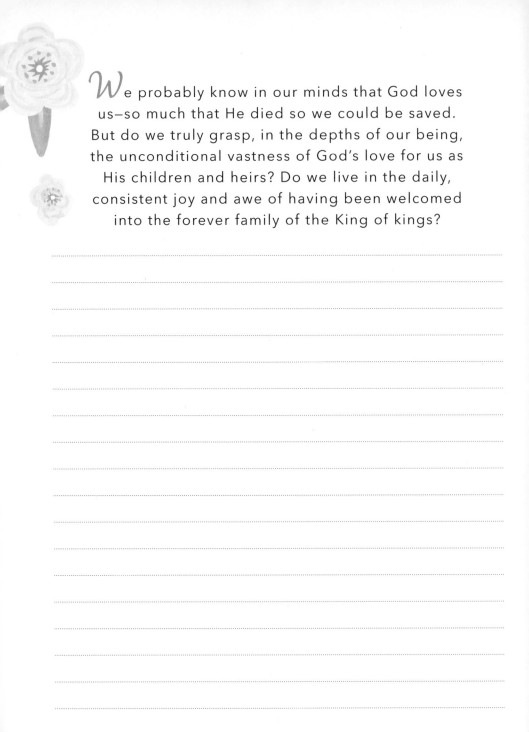

*W*e probably know in our minds that God loves us—so much that He died so we could be saved. But do we truly grasp, in the depths of our being, the unconditional vastness of God's love for us as His children and heirs? Do we live in the daily, consistent joy and awe of having been welcomed into the forever family of the King of kings?

*For you are all children of God through faith in Christ Jesus.
And all who have been united with Christ in baptism have
put on Christ, like putting on new clothes.*

GALATIANS 3:26-27 NLT

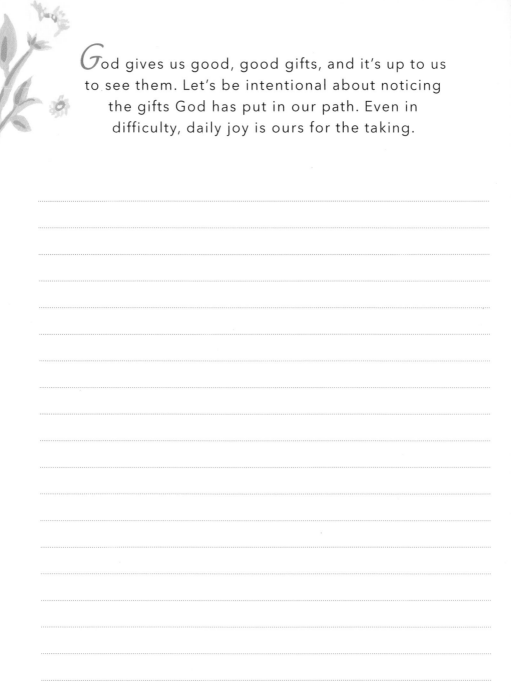

*G*od gives us good, good gifts, and it's up to us to see them. Let's be intentional about noticing the gifts God has put in our path. Even in difficulty, daily joy is ours for the taking.

And so I tell you, keep on asking, and you will receive what you ask for. Keep on seeking, and you will find. Keep on knocking, and the door will be opened to you. For everyone who asks, receives. Everyone who seeks, finds. And to everyone who knocks, the door will be opened. You fathers—if your children ask for a fish, do you give them a snake instead? Or if they ask for an egg, do you give them a scorpion? Of course not! So if you sinful people know how to give good gifts to your children, how much more will your heavenly Father give the Holy Spirit to those who ask him.

LUKE 11:9-13 NLT

The bedrock of joy is coming to grips, in the deepest parts of our being, with God's goodness, majesty, power, and love.

_____

_____

_____

_____

_____

_____

_____

_____

_____

_____

_____

_____

_____

_____

_____

_____

_____

_____

_____

_____

Yours, O LORD, is the greatness and the power and the glory and the victory and the majesty, for all that is in the heavens and in the earth is yours. Yours is the kingdom, O LORD, and you are exalted as head above all.

1 CHRONICLES 29:11 ESV

It is one thing to cry out about how mighty and strong and powerful a king is. It is quite another to worship Him. This awe-inspiring God is not only mighty and glorious: He is GOOD. He is worthy of our worship.

Christ is the visible image of the invisible God. He existed before anything was created and is supreme over all creation, for through him God created everything in the heavenly realms and on earth. He made the things we can see and the things we can't see—such as thrones, kingdoms, rulers, and authorities in the unseen world. Everything was created through him and for him. He existed before anything else, and he holds all creation together.

COLOSSIANS 1:15-17 NLT

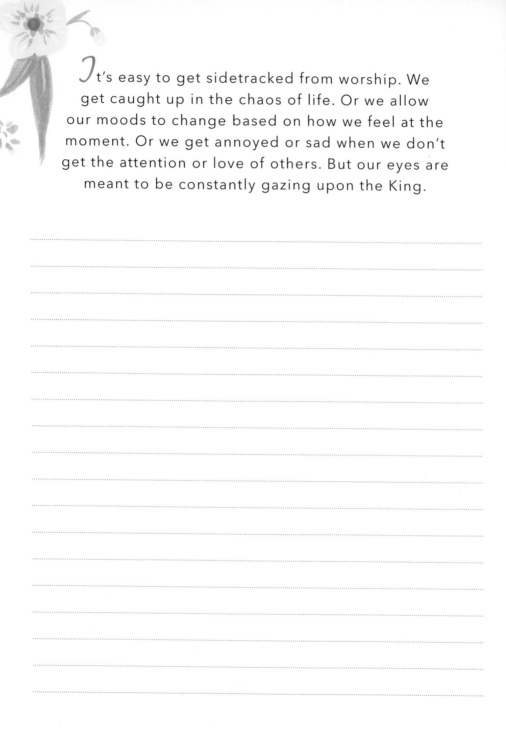

It's easy to get sidetracked from worship. We get caught up in the chaos of life. Or we allow our moods to change based on how we feel at the moment. Or we get annoyed or sad when we don't get the attention or love of others. But our eyes are meant to be constantly gazing upon the King.

Great and marvelous are your deeds, Lord God Almighty. Just and true are your ways, King of the nations. Who will not fear you, Lord, and bring glory to your name? For you alone are holy. All nations will come and worship before you, for your righteous acts have been revealed.

REVELATION 15:3-4 NIV

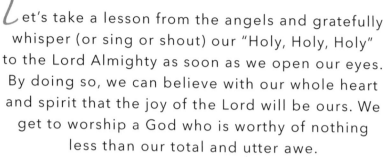

Let's take a lesson from the angels and gratefully whisper (or sing or shout) our "Holy, Holy, Holy" to the Lord Almighty as soon as we open our eyes. By doing so, we can believe with our whole heart and spirit that the joy of the Lord will be ours. We get to worship a God who is worthy of nothing less than our total and utter awe.

The steadfast love of the LORD never ceases; his mercies never come to an end; they are new every morning; great is your faithfulness. "The LORD is my portion," says my soul, "therefore I will hope in him."

LAMENTATIONS 3:22-24 ESV

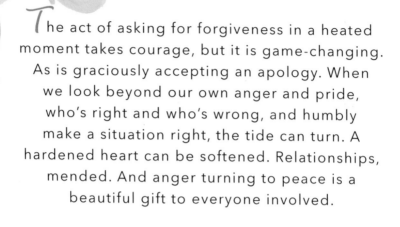

The act of asking for forgiveness in a heated moment takes courage, but it is game-changing. As is graciously accepting an apology. When we look beyond our own anger and pride, who's right and who's wrong, and humbly make a situation right, the tide can turn. A hardened heart can be softened. Relationships, mended. And anger turning to peace is a beautiful gift to everyone involved.

Let all bitterness and wrath and anger and clamor and slander be put away from you, along with all malice. Be kind to one another, tenderhearted, forgiving one another, as God in Christ forgave you.

EPHESIANS 4:31-32 ESV

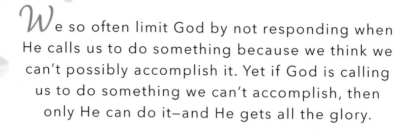

$\mathcal{W}$e so often limit God by not responding when He calls us to do something because we think we can't possibly accomplish it. Yet if God is calling us to do something we can't accomplish, then only He can do it—and He gets all the glory.

We now have this light shining in our hearts, but we ourselves are like fragile clay jars containing this great treasure. This makes it clear that our great power is from God, not from ourselves.

2 CORINTHIANS 4:7 NLT

*I*f you sense God calling you to take a "next step," take it. Watch for the next step . . . and then the next. Pray and wait. No matter what ends up happening, what a privilege it is to watch His plan unfold!

*I will instruct you and teach you in
the way you should go; I will counsel
you with my eye upon you.*

PSALM 32:8 ESV

The good things of the past reassure us of beauty in our future. More important, holding on to memories of adventures, victories, precious moments, and milestones builds our faith.

Only be careful, and watch yourselves closely so that you do not forget the things your eyes have seen or let them fade from your heart as long as you live. Teach them to your children and to their children after them.

DEUTERONOMY 4:9 NIV

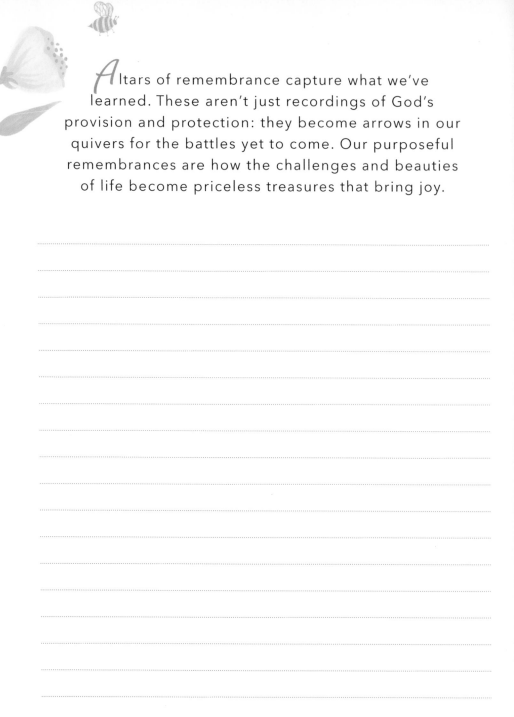

*A*ltars of remembrance capture what we've learned. These aren't just recordings of God's provision and protection: they become arrows in our quivers for the battles yet to come. Our purposeful remembrances are how the challenges and beauties of life become priceless treasures that bring joy.

Oh, magnify the LORD with me, and let us exalt his name together! I sought the LORD, and he answered me and delivered me from all my fears. Those who look to him are radiant, and their faces shall never be ashamed. This poor man cried, and the LORD heard him and saved him out of all his troubles. The angel of the LORD encamps around those who fear him, and delivers them.

PSALM 34:3-7 ESV

*H*is ways are far higher than we can understand. God is great. Our greatest doubt, though, isn't really about God's greatness. It is about His goodness—about whether, when facing something we can't possibly comprehend, we choose to cling to a heavenly Father who loved us enough to send His Son to die for us.

*He who did not spare his own Son but gave him up for us all,
how will he not also with him graciously give us all things?*

ROMANS 8:32 ESV

We need the reminder: God cares.
We will not always know His ways, but
we can know His character.

_____

_____

_____

_____

_____

_____

_____

_____

_____

_____

_____

_____

_____

_____

_____

_____

The rain and snow come down from the heavens and stay on the ground to water the earth. They cause the grain to grow, producing seed for the farmer and bread for the hungry. It is the same with my word. I send it out, and it always produces fruit. It will accomplish all I want it to, and it will prosper everywhere I send it. You will live in joy and peace. The mountains and hills will burst into song, and the trees of the field will clap their hands!

ISAIAH 55:10-12 NLT

*Y*es, our wilderness might still stretch before us. But imagine the difference if we lift our eyes to the free horizon each morning and say, "O God! Thank you that we are here instead of the many harder places we could be!" Each day, we can notice and marvel at the "manna" God provides for us.

The LORD your God, who is going before you, will fight
for you, as he did for you in Egypt, before your very
eyes, and in the wilderness. There you saw how the
LORD your God carried you, as a father carries his son,
all the way you went until you reached this place.

DEUTERONOMY 1:30-31 NIV

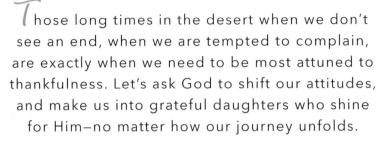

*T*hose long times in the desert when we don't see an end, when we are tempted to complain, are exactly when we need to be most attuned to thankfulness. Let's ask God to shift our attitudes, and make us into grateful daughters who shine for Him—no matter how our journey unfolds.

Rejoice in the Lord always. I will say it again: Rejoice! Let your gentleness be evident to all. The Lord is near. Do not be anxious about anything, but in every situation, by prayer and petition, with thanksgiving, present your requests to God. And the peace of God, which transcends all understanding, will guard your hearts and your minds in Christ Jesus.

PHILIPPIANS 4:4-7 NIV

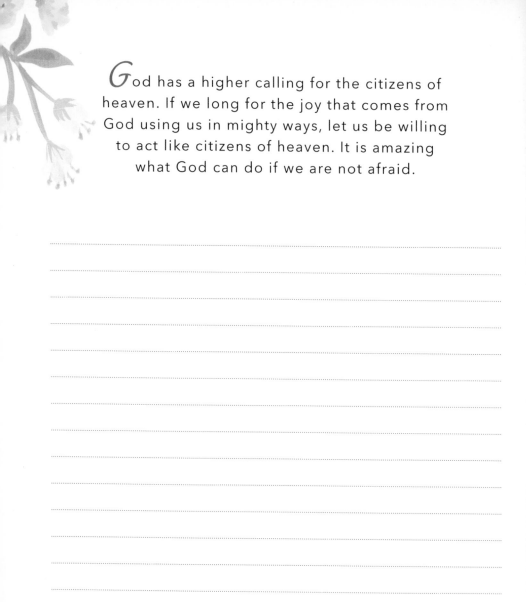

*G*od has a higher calling for the citizens of heaven. If we long for the joy that comes from God using us in mighty ways, let us be willing to act like citizens of heaven. It is amazing what God can do if we are not afraid.

For we know that if the tent that is our earthly home is destroyed, we have a building from God, a house not made with hands, eternal in the heavens.

2 CORINTHIANS 5:1 ESV

*W*e are end-time warriors, with a much higher purpose than just our daily lives: to work on behalf of another Kingdom and undermine the evil forces seeking to steal, kill, and destroy.

Be alert and of sober mind. Your enemy the devil prowls around like a roaring lion looking for someone to devour. Resist him, standing firm in the faith, because you know that the family of believers throughout the world is undergoing the same kind of sufferings. And the God of all grace, who called you to his eternal glory in Christ, after you have suffered a little while, will himself restore you and make you strong, firm and steadfast.

1 PETER 5:8-10 NIV

*W*e are special forces agents with a special calling, and in the field we will have fiery trials. We will face persecution. And we should count it all joy because it is all part of a much, much greater ultimate purpose—something we were built for. Our trials here will seem so short and fleeting when compared to the delight of eternity.

For the LORD your God is living among you. He is a mighty savior. He will take delight in you with gladness. With his love, he will calm all your fears. He will rejoice over you with joyful songs.

ZEPHANIAH 3:17 NLT

*G*od has certain boundaries that He has put in place for our own good. They are His way of saying, "Don't go there or you're going to fall off a cliff! This guardrail is here for your protection. It's not there to hem you in or hold you back in a bad way, but in a good way—because I care about your well-being and because I love you."

Reverence for the LORD is pure, lasting forever. The laws of the LORD are true; each one is fair. They are more desirable than gold, even the finest gold. They are sweeter than honey, even honey dripping from the comb. They are a warning to your servant, a great reward for those who obey them.

PSALM 19:9-11 NLT

$\mathcal{W}$e always need to be willing to take an honest look at whether we are living in "folly"—in ways we know are unwise and wrong. And if we are, then we must be willing to repent, get back on the road, and reestablish honoring those guardrails.

*Foolishness brings joy to those with no sense;
a sensible person stays on the right path.*

PROVERBS 15:21 NLT

In this life, every Christian walks through the valley of betrayal. The enemy always wants to dangle the bait of bitterness. Choosing to truly forgive someone who has devastated us is one of the hardest things we can ever do. Yet it is the only path to having our joy restored. It also brings us to an entirely new level of maturity in God's Kingdom. We all want to be found faithful . . . but the path to get there goes through the profound choice to forgive.

*But love your enemies, and do good, and lend,
expecting nothing in return, and your reward will
be great, and you will be [daughters] of the Most
High, for he is kind to the ungrateful and the evil.
Be merciful, even as your Father is merciful.*

LUKE 6:35-36 ESV

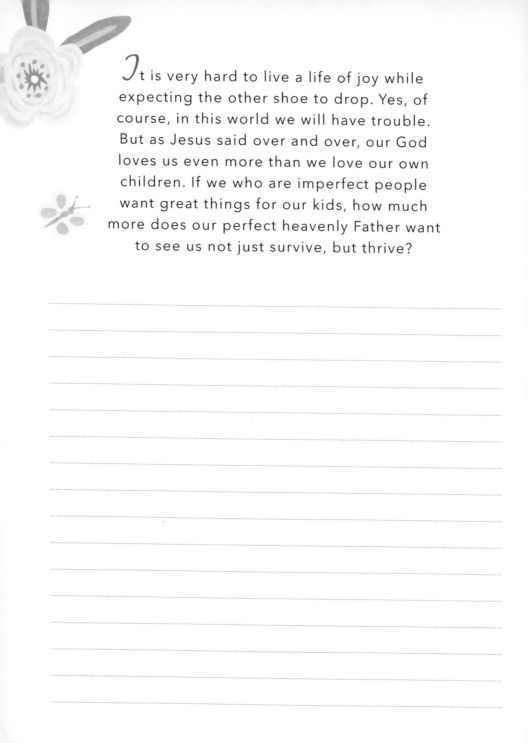

It is very hard to live a life of joy while expecting the other shoe to drop. Yes, of course, in this world we will have trouble. But as Jesus said over and over, our God loves us even more than we love our own children. If we who are imperfect people want great things for our kids, how much more does our perfect heavenly Father want to see us not just survive, but thrive?

*If you then, who are evil, know how to give good gifts
to your children, how much more will your Father who
is in heaven give good things to those who ask him!*

MATTHEW 7:11 ESV

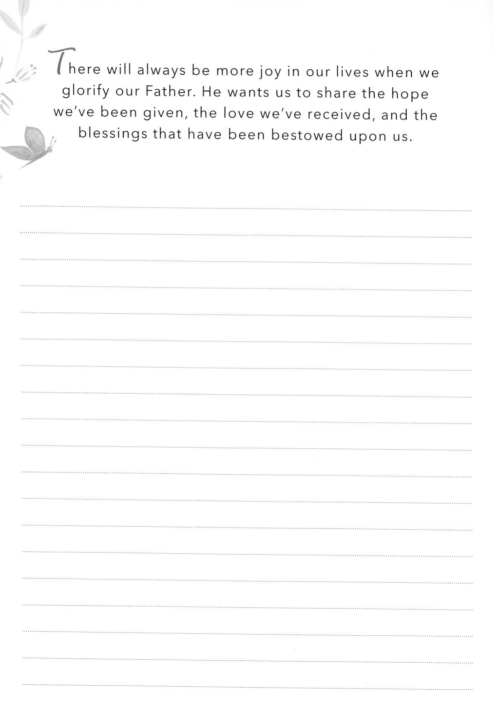

There will always be more joy in our lives when we glorify our Father. He wants us to share the hope we've been given, the love we've received, and the blessings that have been bestowed upon us.

*Therefore be imitators of God, as beloved children.
And walk in love, as Christ loved us and gave himself
up for us, a fragrant offering and sacrifice to God.*

EPHESIANS 5:1-2 ESV

In His presence there is fullness of joy.

You make known to me the path of life; in your presence there is fullness of joy; at your right hand are pleasures forevermore.

PSALM 16:11 ESV

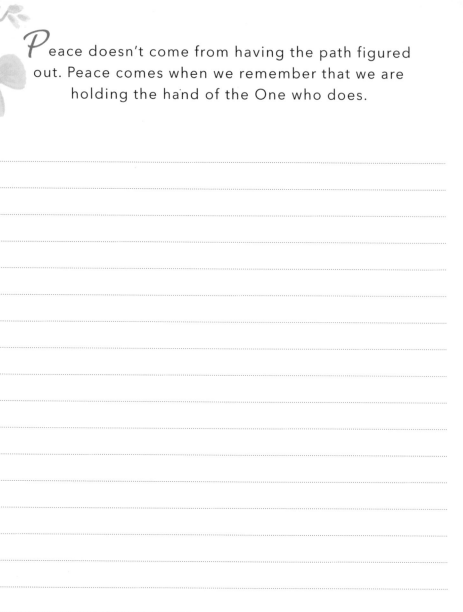

*P*eace doesn't come from having the path figured out. Peace comes when we remember that we are holding the hand of the One who does.

Peace I leave with you; my peace I give you. I do not give to you as the world gives. Do not let your hearts be troubled and do not be afraid.

JOHN 14:27 NIV

God's ways are miraculous. A true moment of service that touches someone else's heart can refresh ours.

*But whoever would be great among you must be your servant,
and whoever would be first among you must be your slave,
even as the Son of Man came not to be served but to serve,
and to give his life as a ransom for many.*

MATTHEW 20:26-28 ESV

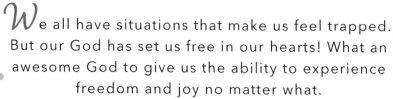

We all have situations that make us feel trapped. But our God has set us free in our hearts! What an awesome God to give us the ability to experience freedom and joy no matter what.

_____

_____

_____

_____

_____

_____

_____

_____

_____

_____

_____

_____

_____

_____

_____

_____

For the Lord is the Spirit, and wherever the Spirit of the Lord is, there is freedom.

2 CORINTHIANS 3:17 NLT

*I*f God is our shepherd, we should always be content to stay by Him, never wandering away to other shepherds. How often do we take something besides God and try to make it our true shepherd? Although health, parenting, and self-improvement are not bad goals, they make terrible shepherds. Earthly masters cater to what we want, but they can never know what we truly need.

*I am the good shepherd. The good shepherd
lays down his life for the sheep.*

JOHN 10:11 NIV

*O*h, the riches of recognizing that our
Good Shepherd knows what we need,
and He gives us exactly that.

The Lord is my shepherd; I shall not want.

PSALM 23:1 ESV

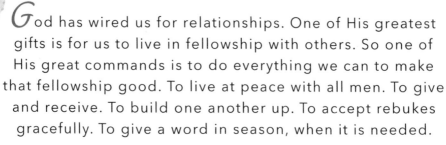

God has wired us for relationships. One of His greatest gifts is for us to live in fellowship with others. So one of His great commands is to do everything we can to make that fellowship good. To live at peace with all men. To give and receive. To build one another up. To accept rebukes gracefully. To give a word in season, when it is needed.

*If it is possible, as far as it depends
on you, live at peace with everyone.*

ROMANS 12:18 NIV

*G*od calls us to mourn with others when the time comes. In a time of great sorrow or hardship, serving others is such an important bridge to the inexplicable, profound "Joy of the Lord" that does not change with circumstances.

*Whoever brings blessing will be enriched, and
one who waters will [herself] be watered.*

PROVERBS 11:25 ESV

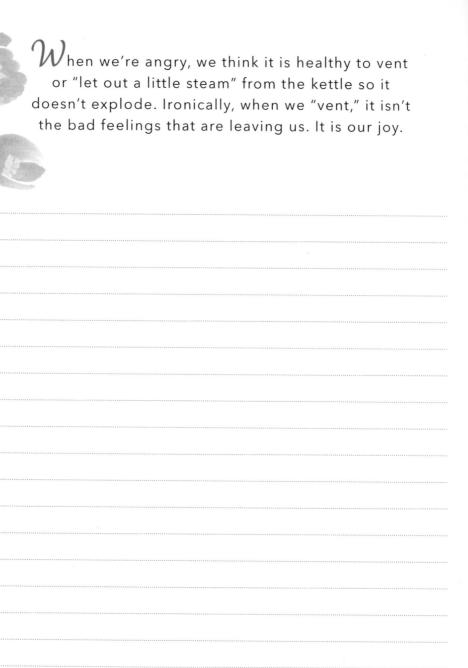

$\mathcal{W}$hen we're angry, we think it is healthy to vent or "let out a little steam" from the kettle so it doesn't explode. Ironically, when we "vent," it isn't the bad feelings that are leaving us. It is our joy.

Always be humble and gentle. Be patient with each other, making allowance for each other's faults because of your love. Make every effort to keep yourselves united in the Spirit, binding yourselves together with peace.

EPHESIANS 4:2-3 NLT

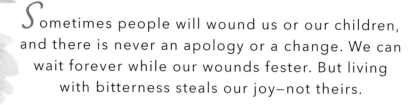

S ometimes people will wound us or our children, and there is never an apology or a change. We can wait forever while our wounds fester. But living with bitterness steals our joy—not theirs.

Don't repay evil for evil. Don't retaliate with insults when people insult you. Instead, pay them back with a blessing. That is what God has called you to do, and he will grant you his blessing.

1 PETER 3:9 NLT

*S*ubmitting to authority is a crucial way that God has provided to grow and mature us and give us true joy. Boundaries do far more than keep us from our own destructive folly. They also temper our pride. They force us to confront our destructive desire to do things our way.

Obey your leaders and submit to them, for they are keeping watch over your souls, as those who will have to give an account. Let them do this with joy and not with groaning, for that would be of no advantage to you.

HEBREWS 13:17 ESV

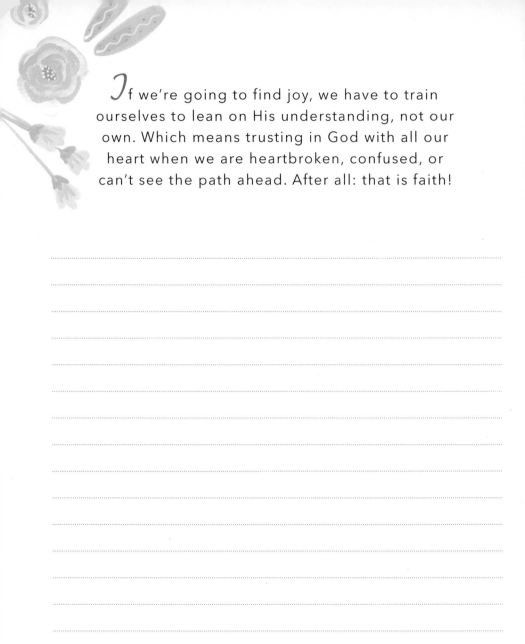

$\mathcal{I}$f we're going to find joy, we have to train ourselves to lean on His understanding, not our own. Which means trusting in God with all our heart when we are heartbroken, confused, or can't see the path ahead. After all: that is faith!

*So don't worry about these things, saying, "What will
we eat? What will we drink? What will we wear?" These
things dominate the thoughts of unbelievers, but your
heavenly Father already knows all your needs. Seek the
Kingdom of God above all else, and live righteously, and
he will give you everything you need.*

MATTHEW 6:31-33 NLT

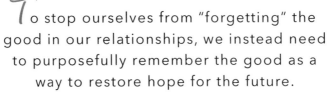

*T*o stop ourselves from "forgetting" the good in our relationships, we instead need to purposefully remember the good as a way to restore hope for the future.

And now, dear brothers and sisters, one final thing.
Fix your thoughts on what is true, and honorable,
and right, and pure, and lovely, and admirable. Think
about things that are excellent and worthy of praise.

PHILIPPIANS 4:8 NLT

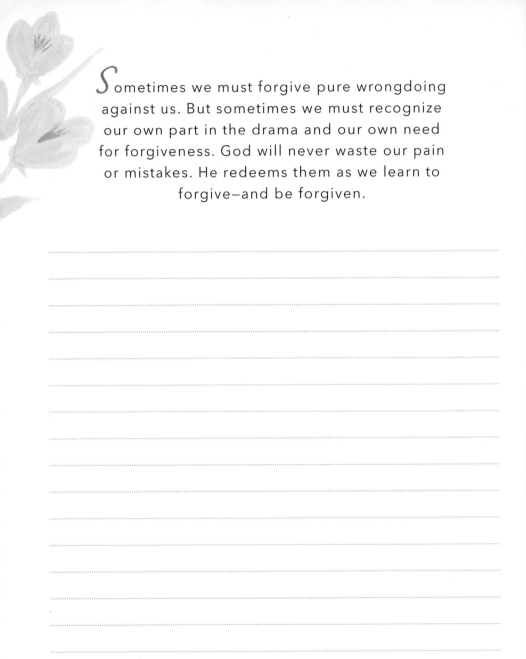

*S*ometimes we must forgive pure wrongdoing
against us. But sometimes we must recognize
our own part in the drama and our own need
for forgiveness. God will never waste our pain
or mistakes. He redeems them as we learn to
forgive—and be forgiven.

For everyone has sinned; we all fall short of God's glorious standard. Yet God, in his grace, freely makes us right in his sight. He did this through Christ Jesus when he freed us from the penalty for our sins.

ROMANS 3:23-24 NLT

*I*t is easy to get distracted and miss that still, small whisper. And yet God is still there, still speaking. Let us recognize our deep need for His direction, every day, on what we should do NOW, and trust that when it is needed, we will hear Him.

My sheep hear my voice, and I know them, and they follow me.

JOHN 10:27 ESV

Our God speaks hope in times that seem hopeless. He provides a promise when our world has completely changed—a promise that He overcomes the darkness. And that message is explosive. It is why the gospel, as seen in the lives of persecuted, loving, joyful people, spread throughout the world.

*I praise God for what he has promised. I
trust in God, so why should I be afraid?
What can mere mortals do to me?*

PSALM 56:4 NLT

$\mathcal{W}$e cannot fathom God's ways. But sometimes we glimpse how He uses even the unfathomably hard times. In the midst of unspeakable pain, unspeakable joy.

....

....

....

....

....

....

....

....

....

....

....

....

....

For thus says the LORD: When seventy years are completed for Babylon, I will visit you, and I will fulfill to you my promise and bring you back to this place. For I know the plans I have for you, declares the LORD, plans for welfare and not for evil, to give you a future and a hope. Then you will call upon me and come and pray to me, and I will hear you. You will seek me and find me, when you seek me with all your heart. I will be found by you, declares the LORD, and I will restore your fortunes and gather you from all the nations and all the places where I have driven you, declares the LORD, and I will bring you back to the place from which I sent you into exile.

JEREMIAH 29:10-14 ESV

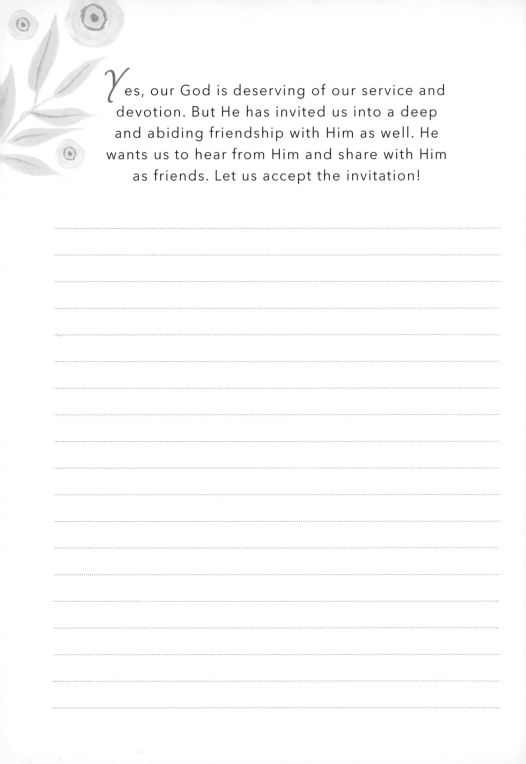

*Y*es, our God is deserving of our service and devotion. But He has invited us into a deep and abiding friendship with Him as well. He wants us to hear from Him and share with Him as friends. Let us accept the invitation!

You see that faith was active along with his works, and faith was completed by his works; and the Scripture was fulfilled that says, "Abraham believed God, and it was counted to him as righteousness"—and he was called a friend of God.

JAMES 2:22-23 ESV

When we are in a season of waiting or worry, it is so easy for our anxious hearts to cling to a particular hope as if it is a promise from God. Which means we risk being devastated if God does not deliver what we want. Yet at the exact same time, our God has made many explosive, life-transforming promises that are real. We must cling to those!

*When you pass through the waters, I will be with you;
and through the rivers, they shall not overwhelm you;
when you walk through fire you shall not be burned, and
the flame shall not consume you. For I am the LORD your
God, the Holy One of Israel, your Savior.*

ISAIAH 43:2-3 ESV

*J*oy rises up once we recognize that God has great power and a great plan that overshadows any heartache this world can throw at us. God is a God of big promises.

But do not overlook this one fact, beloved, that with the Lord one day is as a thousand years, and a thousand years as one day. The Lord is not slow to fulfill his promise as some count slowness, but is patient toward you, not wishing that any should perish, but that all should reach repentance.

2 PETER 3:8-9 ESV

*G*od is always working behind the scenes. He always hears our prayers. He may not always answer them in the way we would like, but He always hears us and comes near to us. He can also bring joy even in the most miserable places, especially when we give thanks in faith while not being able to imagine how God could use something for His purposes—and watch for what God might be doing in the midst of it all.

No, in all these things we are more than conquerors through him who loved us. For I am sure that neither death nor life, nor angels nor rulers, nor things present nor things to come, nor powers, nor height nor depth, nor anything else in all creation, will be able to separate us from the love of God in Christ Jesus our Lord.

ROMANS 8:37-39 ESV

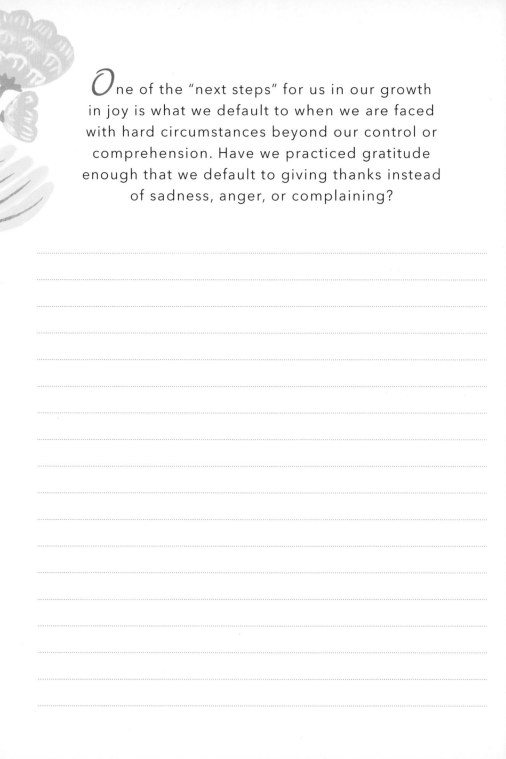

*O*ne of the "next steps" for us in our growth in joy is what we default to when we are faced with hard circumstances beyond our control or comprehension. Have we practiced gratitude enough that we default to giving thanks instead of sadness, anger, or complaining?

And so, dear brothers and sisters, I plead with you to give your bodies to God because of all he has done for you. Let them be a living and holy sacrifice—the kind he will find acceptable. This is truly the way to worship him. Don't copy the behavior and customs of this world, but let God transform you into a new person by changing the way you think. Then you will learn to know God's will for you, which is good and pleasing and perfect.

ROMANS 12:1-2 NLT

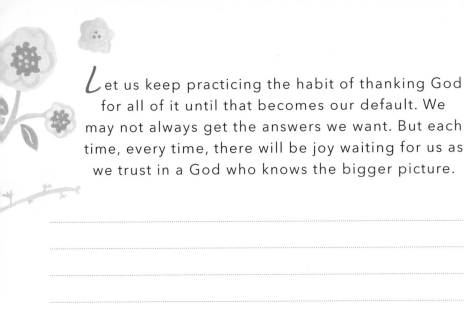

*L*et us keep practicing the habit of thanking God for all of it until that becomes our default. We may not always get the answers we want. But each time, every time, there will be joy waiting for us as we trust in a God who knows the bigger picture.

*I have told you all this so that you may have peace in me.
Here on earth you will have many trials and sorrows. But
take heart, because I have overcome the world.*

JOHN 16:33 NLT

God wants us to steward our gifts well. Our family, our time, our schedules, and even our to-do lists are gifts from God to us. They are meant to be enjoyed.

_____
_____
_____
_____
_____
_____
_____
_____
_____
_____
_____
_____
_____
_____
_____
_____
_____
_____

Each of you should use whatever gift you have received to serve others, as faithful stewards of God's grace in its various forms. If anyone speaks, they should do so as one who speaks the very words of God. If anyone serves, they should do so with the strength God provides, so that in all things God may be praised through Jesus Christ. To him be the glory and the power for ever and ever. Amen.

1 PETER 4:10-12 NIV

The Bible is our road map and guide to a depth of beauty in our relationship with God that is almost inexplicable. Many verses act as signposts to finding that joy. And when we experience that joy even in the face of sorrow or uncertainty, there is simply nothing like it. It is truly a mystery—a gift from God.

Not only that, but we rejoice in our sufferings, knowing that suffering produces endurance, and endurance produces character, and character produces hope, and hope does not put us to shame, because God's love has been poured into our hearts through the Holy Spirit who has been given to us.

ROMANS 5:3-5 ESV

As much as we are called to pursue and find joy here, this world is not our home. Here, our joy will inevitably be shadowed. But in eternity, in the presence of God, there will be no shadows. There will be none of the pain and loss that stalks our world.

*He will wipe away every tear from their eyes,
and death shall be no more, neither shall there
be mourning, nor crying, nor pain anymore, for
the former things have passed away.*

REVELATION 21:4 ESV

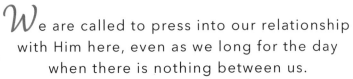

$\mathcal{W}$e are called to press into our relationship
with Him here, even as we long for the day
when there is nothing between us.

....
....
....
....
....
....
....
....
....
....
....
....
....
....
....
....

So we are always confident, even though we know that as long as we live in these bodies we are not at home with the Lord. For we live by believing and not by seeing. Yes, we are fully confident, and we would rather be away from these earthly bodies, for then we will be at home with the Lord. So whether we are here in this body or away from this body, our goal is to please him.

2 CORINTHIANS 5:6-9 NLT

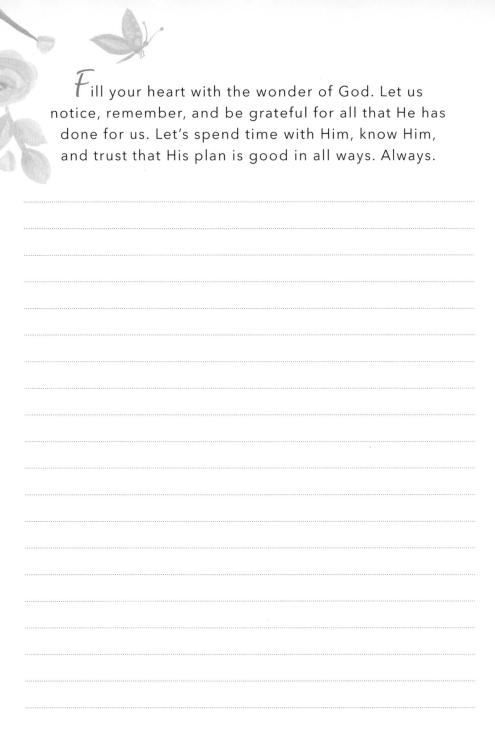

*F*ill your heart with the wonder of God. Let us notice, remember, and be grateful for all that He has done for us. Let's spend time with Him, know Him, and trust that His plan is good in all ways. Always.

Make a joyful noise to the LORD, all the earth! Serve the LORD with gladness! Come into his presence with singing! Know that the LORD, he is God! It is he who made us, and we are his; we are his people, and the sheep of his pasture. Enter his gates with thanksgiving, and his courts with praise! Give thanks to him; bless his name! For the LORD is good; his steadfast love endures forever, and his faithfulness to all generations.

PSALM 100:1-5 ESV